IN TUNE WITH TRADITION

Wisconsin Folk Musical Instruments

Extensive inlay work and
delicate India ink
"rosing" decorate the
hardanger fiddles of
Ron Poast, Black Earth,
Wisconsin.

IN TUNE WITH TRADITION

Wisconsin Folk Musical Instruments

FIELD RESEARCH AND CATALOGUE ESSAY
by James P. Leary

PHOTOGRAPHY
by Lewis Koch

CURATED AND EDITED
by Robert T. Teske

A TRAVELING EXHIBITION ORGANIZED BY THE
Cedarburg Cultural Center   Cedarburg, Wisconsin

*Funded in part by grants from the Wisconsin Arts Board
and the National Endowment for the Arts*

Published in conjunction with a traveling exhibition organized
and presented by the Cedarburg Cultural Center, Cedarburg,
Wisconsin, March 18 - June 2, 1990.

All photographs included in this publication, unless otherwise
indicated in the captions, are © Lewis Koch and used by permission.

Designed by Victor DiCristo, DiCristo Slagle Design, Milwaukee.
Printed by Schroeder Printing, Cedarburg.
Printed in the United States of America.

EXHIBITION TOUR

March 18 - June 2, 1990	Cedarburg Cultural Center Cedarburg, Wisconsin
June 16 - July 27, 1990	Wriston Art Center Lawrence University Appleton, Wisconsin
September 18, 1990 - January 13, 1991	State Historical Museum Madison, Wisconsin
February 25 - March 29, 1991	New Visions Gallery Marshfield, Wisconsin
April 15 - October 31, 1991	Chippewa Valley Museum Eau Claire, Wisconsin

TABLE OF CONTENTS

A traveling exhibition of the size and scope of IN TUNE WITH TRADITION: WISCONSIN FOLK MUSICAL INSTRUMENTS could not be organized and presented without the assistance and cooperation of a large number of dedicated individuals and collaborating organizations. The Board of Directors of the Cedarburg Cultural Center wishes to extend its sincere appreciation to the many who have helped our young organization carry out this complex and challenging project.

First of all, we wish to thank the Wisconsin Arts Board and the Folk Arts Program of the National Endowment for the Arts for providing generous financial support for IN TUNE WITH TRADITION. The staffs of both funding agencies, particularly Richard March of the Arts Board and Bess Lomax Hawes and Barry Bergey of the Endowment, were especially helpful in the early stages of planning the project.

Secondly, we wish to acknowledge the exceptional fieldwork carried out in preparation for the exhibition by folklorist James P. Leary and photographer Lewis Koch. The words and images included in the exhibit and catalogue are largely the product of their extraordinary efforts at seeking out and documenting Wisconsin's folk instrument-makers. We also wish to thank the many experts in Wisconsin folk music who have advised us in the development of the project. Dr. Thomas Vennum, Jr. of the Smithsonian Institution, Phil Martin of the Wisconsin Folk Museum, Dr. Nancy Lurie of the Milwaukee Public Museum, and Cecil Negron of the Social Development Commission in Milwaukee have provided invaluable assistance in their areas of expertise.

Thirdly, the Cultural Center's Board of Directors wishes to thank the many institutions throughout Wisconsin which have assisted in various ways with the development and presentation of IN TUNE WITH TRADITION. The State Historical Museum in Madison has generously contributed the expertise of its staff to the planning and fabrication of the exhibition. Special thanks are due Director William Crowley, Exhibition Curator David Mandel, and Education Curator Howard

ACKNOWLEDGEMENTS

Kanetzke. The State Historical Society in Madison, the Milwaukee Public Museum, the Wisconsin Folk Museum in Mt. Horeb, the Rusk County Historical Society in Ladysmith, and Vesterheim, the Norwegian-American Museum in Decorah, Iowa, have graciously loaned objects and photographs from their collections for inclusion in the exhibition. Their cooperation is deeply appreciated. In addition, the Wriston Art Center of Lawrence University in Appleton, the State Historical Museum in Madison, New Visions Gallery in Marshfield, and the Chippewa Valley Museum in Eau Claire have agreed to present IN TUNE WITH TRADITION to audiences in other parts of the state. For their generous cooperation and support we are most grateful.

         Fourthly, the Cultural Center Board wishes to recognize our organization's many volunteers for their invaluable assistance in organizing and presenting this exhibition. The required tasks involved in this presentation—painting display panels, assembling cases, typing labels, and mailing invitations—could not have been accomplished without our loyal volunteers. To all of you, our friends and neighbors in Cedarburg, a heartfelt "thank you."

         Finally, the Cedarburg Cultural Center wishes to extend its sincerest thanks to the folk musical instrument-makers of Wisconsin whose work is the reason for this exhibition. All of the instrument-makers included in the exhibition have been generous in sharing their time and expertise during the field research phase of the project. They have been more than generous in creating and loaning their instruments for the eighteen-month tour of IN TUNE WITH TRADITION. For their kindness and consideration, and for all they do to enhance the rich quality of life here in Wisconsin, we thank them sincerely.

Carl W. Edquist
President
Cedarburg Cultural Center

Throughout Wisconsin's history, traditional music has been an important element in the daily life of many of the state's ethnic, regional and occupational communities. Among Wisconsin's Indians, songs were believed to provide a link with the spirit world, and the measured beat of dance drums provided accompaniment to ritual and ceremonial. In Wisconsin's north woods during the logging boom of the late nineteenth and early twentieth centuries, fiddle tunes, button accordion music and ballads of brave lumberjacks were among the only entertainments available to the men in the isolated lumber camps. Within Wisconsin's numerous ethnic communities, folksongs performed in German or Polish, Norwegian or Italian reminded singers of home and family, national identity and cultural heritage.

The instruments which have accompanied and given voice to the music of Wisconsin's folk communities over the years have often been the creations of individual craftspeople living and working in those very communities. Some have taken up instrument-making because of the sound. Musicians themselves, many instrument-makers have fashioned flutes and fiddles for their own personal use. Others have been drawn to building instruments by the sight of these beautiful works of art. Accomplished craftworkers with a feel for wood, an eye for design, and an appreciation of function, they have found instrument-making an exciting challenge. Still others have turned to crafting folk musical instruments because they are such important symbols. Children of earlier instrument-makers or members of ethnic communities with a proud musical heritage, they have assumed the responsibility for continuing a valued family or cultural tradition and passing it along to another generation. The legacy of Wisconsin's earlier instrument-makers, its "past masters," persists today in the extraordinary work of a number of folk artists. In communities throughout the state, they continue to create Ojibwa dance drums and Woodland flutes, hardanger fiddles and Croatian tamburitzas, Greek bouzoukis and Italian accordions. Instrument-makers from older, more established communities have also been joined by recent immigrants who strive to keep alive their folk musical traditions. Puerto Rican and Hmong instrument-makers, for example, have added *cuatros* and bamboo flutes to the range of musical instruments currently crafted in Wisconsin. Working at home or in workshops behind family-owned stores, these gifted individuals fashion instruments which are objects of art in themselves and which enrich the lives of all Wisconsin residents by making possible the continued performance of the state's many and varied forms of folk music.

Robert T. Teske
Director
Cedarburg Cultural Center

WISCONSIN FOLK MUSICAL INSTRUMENTS:
OBJECTS, SOUNDS, AND SYMBOLS

Stylized solar patterns
adorn the soundboards
of Konstantins Dravnieks'
Latvian *kokles*.

INTRODUCTION

On a late Spring morning in Rice Lake, Wisconsin, perhaps 1957, I was thrilled by the gift of a willow whistle, newly carved by the German grandfather of my neighbor, Greg Rothe. A pair of noisy kids, Greg and I went whistling into the woods and down a steep bank to Lake Montanis where Greg tore off a blade of grass, cupped it to his lips, and produced a succession of notes—a practice learned from his grandfather. The leaf was soon tossed away and by summer my whistle was tucked in a drawer where it dried up, lost its tone, and became a mute yet treasured souvenir. Rediscovering it from time to time, I wondered yet never asked where Grandpa Rothe had acquired his wonderful knowledge.

Years later I read that documents dating from the early sixteenth century describe southern German and Swiss children making music on blades of grass and playing "May pipes."

> The most suitable materials are straight pieces from willow, hazel, alder, ash, lilac, or chestnut trees. First a crescent-shaped airhole is made in the bark half an inch from one end. A circular incision is then made around the bark near the other end of the branch. The branch is then tapped all over with the back of a knife and the bark is pulled gently from the wooden core in one piece. Finally, a half-inch long stopper is cut from the wood and is pushed up to the airhole in the bark tube. (Geiser 1976:39)

Across time and space old Leo Rothe fashioned his whistles in the same way, in the same season, and for children.

Many such makers of traditional musical instruments, with lineages as ancient and homelands as distant, flourish in Wisconsin today. While the term "multiculturalism" has newly entered the nation's vocabulary, Wisconsin has always been a multicultural state, a place where peoples of diverse backgrounds have been able to practice and sustain their cultural traditions. Not surprisingly the state's native peoples, its European immigrants, and its African-, Asian-, and Hispanic-American newcomers all include traditional musical instrument-makers.

These makers' works are often far more complex and varied than Grandpa Rothe's simple willow whistles, but like him they all produce something ineffable, something resonant with mysterious power and meaning. That something cannot be captured in prose, although I can offer its crude outlines. Traditional musical instruments are many things at once. Most apparently, they are palpable *objects*, crafted in familiar forms from wood, metal, bits of skin and string. They also become, in the right hands, structured *sounds*—wordless songs from a culture's soul. Finally, as important objects and sounds of a people, traditional musical instruments have often come to serve as *symbols* of the larger essence of that people.

OBJECTS

The successful construction of traditional musical objects requires the acquisition of basic skills, the right materials, an array of specialized tools, a well-developed personal aesthetic regarding technique and design, and an appreciative community. Historically most traditional instruments were made by men who, in keeping with cultural divisions of labor along gender lines, manipulated wood and metal while women excelled in foodways and fiber arts. These men learned their craft informally: by observing some elder, by utilizing local materials, by fashioning their own tools, by following designs that balanced traditionality with creativity, and by serving an entire homogeneous community of musicians, singers, and dancers. While this venerable and classic pattern continues to a degree, Wisconsin's contemporary instrument-makers most typically depart from aspects of it in ways that are, in keeping with late twentieth century society, diverse and complex.

ACQUISITION OF SKILLS

Charles Ackley (1902-1973) learned to make drums in the company of his father, Willard, the last chief of the Mole Lake band of Ojibwas and a member of the *medewiwin* or Grand Medicine Society. The teaching was indirect, informal, incremental, yet bound by specific cultural rules, a method Charles repeated with his son, Joseph. The younger Ackley, who makes drums nowadays for his people when they are needed, remembers his father's instructions:

> *You have to have a drummaker in your family before you follow that. You can't just go and start making drums. I suppose you could, but it's not traditional.*

As a boy Joseph recalls helping his father with the lengthy, smelly process of tanning deer hides for drum heads, then working on the drum's body: "I'd watch him, see how they did it, then finally I started making my own."

Milwaukee's Miguel Cruz similarly gained the rudiments of his craft by observing his father, Juan Cruz, on the farm back home in Aguas Buenas, Puerto Rico. The elder Cruz, like the Ackleys, was a religious man whose ten-stringed *cuatros* figured in seasonal fiestas. By pursuing the craft learned from *his* father, Juan Cruz became *cuatro*-maker *"por el barrio,"* a responsibility Miguel assumed in Wisconsin's Puerto Rican community.

While the youthful apprenticeships of the Ackleys and Miguel Cruz occurred in a loosely structured manner, strictly within the family, and amidst the normal course of everyday life and work, other instrument-makers won their competence during specified hours in factory settings, ascending from simple to difficult tasks. By the mid-nineteenth century the accordion, a central European invention, had become popular throughout Europe. Individual craftsmen, cottage industries, and factories proliferated to meet demand, with the latter dominating by the century's end.

Andrew Karpek spent ten years mastering his trade in Russian Poland before immigrating to Milwaukee in 1911 where he soon established the Karpek Accordion Manufacturing Company. His children, George and Olga, were raised in the shop. Olga Karpek Russell's memoirs recall the pair's first chores: punching holes in reed plates, assembling bellows from cardboard, leather, and colored paper, and glueing black and white celluloid keys in place—a job that required readying "the old iron glue pot...the stench was something terrific and quite a sticky job." (Russell 1975:33)

Alfonso Baldoni of Milwaukee was raised similarly in Castelfidardo, Italy, where his father and grandfather had crafted accordions in the city's world renowned factories. By the time he had risen through the ranks to become a head tuner, he had mastered all the intricacies of accordion construction. Nowadays his son, Ivo, designs, modifies, and repairs accordions and guitars for A. Baldoni Music Service, while Ivo's young son, showered with as many tools as toys, is already beginning his apprenticeship.

Although the pan-European popularity of the accordion and its broad acceptance by ethnic Americans encouraged masters like Karpek and Baldoni to transplant their art from old world to new, no comparable force attracted makers of such esoteric instruments as the bouzouki, the *hardingfela*, or the tamburitza. Meanwhile, makers of the accordion, the related German concertina, and even the fiddle—while common enough in urban Milwaukee—have always been comparatively scarce in Wisconsin's hinterlands. Necessity and ingenuity, consequently, have motivated most of the state's instrument-makers. Typically they are musicians and woodworkers who begin by repairing some treasured but decrepit instrument.

Anton Wolfe, a Bayfield County farmer, began tinkering with concertinas in the early 1940s when his broke and parts from Germany could not be had during wartime. Ray Polarski of Three Lakes commenced at twelve when he traded his labor for fiddling tips.

> *My neighbor, he was a French Canadian...And I repaired a*
> *violin for him. I took part of dad's woodpile apart and I finally*
> *found the right color wood. I was pretty handy at carving. I*
> *carved one out, glued it in...So I decided I was going to make a*
> *fiddle. It was pretty grubby, sounded like one made out of a cigar box.*
> *But I got to work on and repair quite a number of them. And*
> *I got better at it all the time. So that's how I got started.*

Nick Vukusich learned woodworking while summering with his Croatian grandfather in the early 1930s near Mellen. Years later he taught himself to make a tamburitza by disassembling an old one to see how it was made, then using it as a pattern.

While Vukusich and Epaminontas Bourantas—who also took apart an old instrument, a bouzouki, to discover how to make a new one—can be regarded as cultural conservationists protecting "endangered species," others have retrieved musical instruments from near extinction. Books, courses, and archival research have aided Ron Poast, Jim Razer, Louis Webster, and Konstantins Dravnieks.

When Ron Poast was a young boy on a farm near Blue Mounds, he heard stories from his mother about a mysterious eight-stringed fiddle, beautifully inlaid with mother-of-pearl.

> *She didn't know what it was. I didn't know what it was. But*
> *that always stuck in my mind...Maybe ten, twelve years ago, I*
> *was up in Mount Horeb, in one of the shops up there. There*

Fiddler and fiddle-maker Anton Rundhaug of La Crosse posed in traditional costume with his hardanger fiddle during the early 1890s. (Photo courtesy of the Wisconsin Folk Museum, Mt. Horeb.)

> *was one in the window. On display. I looked at it and my eyes*
> *bugged out. That's it! This is the thing my mother was talking about!*
> *And it was a hardanger fiddle.*

Already acquainted with the principles of instrument construction, Poast tracked down a book by Sverre Sandvik in Norwegian on making hardanger fiddles. Aided by a dictionary and Sandvik's pictures and measurements, Poast traveled to the Norwegian-American museum, Vesterheim, in Decorah, Iowa, to examine the actual instruments. "We were making fiddles when we came back."

Jim Razer was systematically cut off from his Ojibwa roots through state schooling in the 1930s. By the late 1950s, however, he had begun to confer with elders, scrutinize museum collections, and study the works of anthropologists in an effort to reconstruct his people's material culture. In the 1970s Louis Webster, a Menominee, followed his introduction to Woodland people's flutes in an anthropology class at the University of Wisconsin-Milwaukee by making them himself. Meanwhile Konstantins Dravnieks of Thiensville, an engineer and Latvian emigre, made precise drawings of kokles in the hands of musicians, collectors, and museums so as to render at least the main features of his own instruments "ethnographically correct."

MATERIALS

Latvian kokles of old were often strung with horsehair, their bodies and pegs were of native maple or basswood, their resonating tops of straight-grained European spruce. But steel strings ring truer in modern ears and Konstantins Dravnieks finds music wire from hardware stores "the simplest, the cheapest, and the best." While he acquires Wisconsin maple and basswood easily from local lumberyards, he also chooses to import costly European spruce, instead of using domestic varieties, for his soundboards. Wooden pegs are the greatest challenge. Temperature and humidity affect body and pegs, making the latter hard to turn and tuning nigh impossible. Rather than accept this situation or abandon traditional wooden pegs for the reliability of metal, Dravnieks prefers a tree that grows neither in Latvian nor Wisconsin forests. South American cocobolo is hard, durable, oily, and retains it shape.

The selection of raw materials by other instrument-makers in Wisconsin involves a similar balancing act between the dictates of traditional practice and the mitigating factors of environment, economics, and personal taste; between the way it was in a bygone folk society and what is "the simplest, the cheapest, and the best" today. Miguel Cruz's father went to the woods on his Puerto Rican farm, cut and cured wood to fashion a cuatro, and boiled down the pinuela plant for glue. Miguel roams Milwaukee's concrete jungle seeking old dressers to recycle their mahogany, white pine, and even plywood into cuatros, holding the parts together with commercial Elmer's Glue.

Such scavenging is typical of newcomers to Wisconsin who often lack the economic wherewithal and knowledge of the territory necessary to procure just the right raw materials. Wang Chou Vang, a Hmong, was unable to find bamboo of the sort grown in Laos to make resonators for his two-stringed violin, the ncauj nrog ncas. He experimented with a metal patio lamp before discovering a gourd that would work. Other Hmong have used Ovaltine tins and coconut shells for resonators.

Perhaps Wisconsin's most prominent scavengers were such "lumberjack" instrument-makers as Otto Rindlisbacher and Ray Calkins who used cigar boxes, broom handles, pitchforks, screen door wire, and what have you. During a performance of the Wisconsin Lumberjacks in the early 1960s, Calkins' fellow musician, Hank Thompson, announced:

> I'm playing the homemade violin that's made by Mr. Calkins.
> It sounds pretty good. It was made out of lumber. He found some
> old board out there in his alley, he says. And he picked it up
> and made a fiddle out of it. And I'm playing it tonight. (Starr 1960s)

Earl Schwartztrauber confessed to plucking a "bangola" or "lumberjack bull fiddle" made from "an old washtub and a piece of plastic clothesline for a string," while Don Calkins' guitar was "made out of just some old pine wood, tin can for a bridge, piece of deer horn for a nut." Ray's "Paul Bunyan Guitar" was similarly constructed.

While the Wisconsin Lumberjacks' proud declaration of their instruments' mongrel pedigree was an extension of occupational pride in material improvisation—in being "handy" fellows, proverbial "jacks-of-all-trades" who could make "something out of anything"—instrument-makers who produce on a relatively large scale have gone out of their way to use precisely the right materials. Bill Schwartz's "Stumpf fiddles" are composed of several discrete sonic parts, one of which is the "Bermuda taxi horn." Available only from Japan, its price has tripled in recent years; yet Schwartz swears by its quality and will not compromise his product with an inferior substitute. Ivo Baldoni similarly defends his preference for top quality materials in Baldoni accordions: "It's like manufacturing your standard automobile *or* a piece of art work, it's like making a Chevrolet *or* a Mercedes."

Most instrument-makers, however, neither scavenge for materials nor go to great expense to import them. They get what they can locally, and send away for what they must. Anton Wolfe uses basswood, birch, and maple from the home farm for concertina boxes. Joe Ackley uses the skins of deer he's hunted for drumheads. Ron Poast prowls lumberyards for the curly maple that forms fiddle backs, as does Louis Webster who reckons he would "be an old man" before he could cut and cure enough wood for his flutes. And Jim Razer gets deer toes from processing plants in hunting season to make jingles. Others purchase strings and pegs at music stores and order ebony, Sitka spruce, and exotic woods from specialty firms catering to instrument-makers.

TOOLS

Those who make only an occasional instrument, or who are trying consciously, like Jim Razer, to keep to the old ways, rely chiefly on hand tools: axes, knives, scrapers, and the like. But even Razer employs a bandsaw in the process of making deer toe jingles. There is little romance or pleasure in elementary, repetitive labor. Whereas an ancestor might have of necessity crafted an entire instrument with hand tools, contemporary artisans like Ron Poast who have, or have access to, power tools use "table saws, coping saws, power sanders" to "rough out" an instrument, then switch to hand tools for "fine work."

Some instrument-makers go so far as to design or modify machines to accomplish specialized but routine tasks. Anton Wolfe tailored die punches for the reed plates on his concertinas, and Stanley Twardowski developed a multi-bladed table saw to cut grooves that simulate bellows in his wooden miniatures of accordions and concertinas. Many others make jigs or patterns for their instruments, be they fiddle, bouzouki, or tamburitza. And nearly all modify or make hand tools for a variety of reasons.

Although he can purchase ready-made gouges for $20

Ray Polarski of Three Lakes holds a form used for shaping his fiddles.

to $30, Ron Poast prefers to buy good steel and grind his own. Whereas scrapers cost $15 each, Poast buys ten sickle teeth for $3, then heat treats, tempers, and grinds them to the curved or rounded shape he needs. Economics figure in his choice, but pride in craftsmanship is perhaps more prominent. Indeed he may be able to buy a gouge or scraper, but not *precisely* the one he must have for his own specialized work.

Apprentice craftsmen of a bygone age had to learn to make their own tools, thereby gaining not only a skill essential to their livelihood, but also a degree of control over implements that are, after all, an extension of their own being. No wonder Ray Polarski beams while showing the tool he has made from a screwdriver handle and a sewing machine needle for faultlessly cutting purfling grooves on his fiddles. No wonder Epaminontas Bourantas delights in the special blade he has fashioned to cut frets of the right width and thickness to accommodate a bouzouki's curved and tapered neck.

DESIGN

Certain traditional instruments vary widely in design and name through time and space, while others remain relatively constant. Bill Schwartz's "Stumpf fiddle" is descended from a family of western European monochords or stick zithers, dubbed variously "according to region, the German name *Bumbass* being commonly adopted in folk instrument literature." (Sadie, vol. 1, 1984: 245) In America, the term "boomba" is most common, but "bumberstick," "polkacello," "humstrum," "*Teufel stick*," "devil's fiddle," and "Paul Bunyan fiddle" are also used. For those not subtle enough to tell the difference, Schwartz is careful to point out that the particular components of his instrument are unique. A boomba made by "a gentleman in Milwaukee," for example, strikes Schwartz as "a completely different instrument."

Ray Polarski and Epaminontas Bourantas, like many other Wisconsin instrument-makers, would not claim their respective fiddles and bouzoukis differ generically from those made by someone else. But each man can tell his work from another's. Indeed both are adept designers, albeit in small ways. The former makes his key welds just a little heavier to hold the pegs, the latter drafts and refines complex blueprints for combining 1,003 distinct parts. Each favors a variety of woods not just for their sound and durability, but for their look and feel: bird's eye and curly maple, black walnut, rosewood, and teak. Bourantas has also tested his designer's mettle by making a half size bouzouki, a *baglama*.

Such incremental tinkering with basic construction techniques, external decoration, and scale typify the design proclivities of Wisconsin's traditional instrument-makers. Neither Hugo Terauds nor Konstantins Dravnieks ever made a *kokle* the same way. Terauds even carved numerals into his instruments the way a visual artist might number related but distinct works in a series. Meanwhile Dravnieks, following his engineer's training, made *kokles* in sets of three, using the same woods, thickness in the soundboard, strings, and pegs on each, but making one of a standard length, one shorter, and one longer. Each instrument was likewise ornamented with varying scrolls and solar motifs.

Part of Dravnieks' fascination with minute changes is the result of his own thorough historical research into the evolving design of the Latvian *kokles*. It is hardly suprising that many instrument-makers are keenly aware of the diversity and antiquity of the traditions they practice. Indeed more than a few enjoy working both within and beyond tradition. Louis

Webster regards himself as a Woodland Indian flute-maker, but also as an artist in his own right.

> *Most of the flutes I make are copies from what I've seen before, but a lot of them are my own designs. I like to experiment with designs. I've made deer legs and eagle heads, woodpeckers, robins, loons, and, of course, different straight flutes.*

The woodpecker flutes are favored by Native American Church members, while those in the bear clan prefer that animal or its paw for a straight flute's saddle. Dreams inspire still other designs. "I dressed one up in claws and fur and a head. It's some kind of animal. I don't know what."

Artistry and business acumen combine in design changes wrought by the Baldonis. They actively seek advice from working accordionists and concertina-players, sometimes building custom squeezeboxes to their specifications. Rather than design for ease of production, the Baldonis take pains to get the best sound from the lightest weight, to ensure that "the spacing of the keys, the lifting of the keys, the response, the folds of the bellow" are just right. Their success as a professional business derives in part from their prowess at extending the capabilities of the accordion.

Autographed photographs of well-known accordionists who favor Baldoni instruments on display in the Milwaukee showroom of A. Baldoni Music Service.

COMMUNITY

Although rooted in Italy and based in Milwaukee, the Baldoni Music Service commands a national clientele. The Baldonis participate in major instrument shows on the west coast and in the Midwest, and they hold perhaps a dozen "jamborees" annually. These events, often drawing in the hundreds, involve virtuoso players demonstrating on assorted products in the Baldoni line: Don Gralak of Milwaukee on concertina; Mike Ashworth of Madison on jazz accordion; Gordon Hartmann of Madison on American polka accordion; and Art Gasch of La Crosse on button accordion. Through vigorous promotion and marketing, the Baldonis have been able to take advantage of the first boom in the accordion business since the onslaught of guitars in the 1950s.

The arrival of rock and roll crimped the cross-town Milwaukee business of the Karpek Accordion Manufacturing Company. Although one of a few such companies in America, and one that attracted business from Chicago, Detroit, and New York, Karpek relied chiefly on the large, steady, ethnic, working-class clientele that bought its instruments and flocked to its accordion schools from the 1920s until the early '50s. More than a business, Karpek's was a "hangout," a place where people could drop in to try out a new instrument or have an old one repaired. Like an old country storekeeper, George Karpek set out chairs so his patrons could sit around, talk, and play music. Nowadays daughter Georjann reckons the customers are mostly old timers and, since George died, the number of chairs and of their occupants has declined.

Traditional instrument-making historically has been grounded in folk communities and their modern extensions: the ethnic enclaves, neighborhoods, extended families, occupational groups of the sort that patronized the Karpek Accordion Manufacturing Company. Particular instruments were crucial to the everyday and ceremonial life of such communities, and they were made because people had to have them for existence to go on as always or, at least, as it used to be. The status of such communities as integral wholes, however, is precarious in contemporary society. Traditional instrument-makers who have continued or newly taken up their art, like the Baldonis, have often had to seek new and complex communities, and those communities in turn are constantly evolving and transforming.

Slovenian dancers and musicians at a picnic in Willard, Wisconsin, 1988. (Photo courtesy of James P. Leary.)

SOUNDS

Continuity and change in traditional instrument-making as a part of community life is inextricably bound with traditional music, with the sounds of instruments, with their players, with those who dance, sing, and listen.

NATIVE PEOPLES

Woodland Indians of the nineteenth century played a narrow array of traditional instruments, all of them inextricable with ceremonial life. Gourd or turtle shell rattles filled with seeds or pebbles, and jingle rattles from the dried dewclaws of deer or moose accompanied the songs of medicine men in curing and ritual. Young men courting played love songs on wooden end-blown flutes. Water drums—hollowed from basswood or cedar, partially filled, with deerskin drumheads—were exclusive to the medicine lodge. Meanwhile tambourine-shaped hand drums had various functions corresponding to their sizes:

the drum used by the medicine man for doctoring was considerably smaller in diameter than that used to accompany gambling songs, which in turn was smaller than the drum a man took on the warpath. (Vennum 1982:31)

The large dance drum mainly in use today emerged only in the late nineteenth century. By then the reservation system, combined with the efforts of government agents and missionaries to assimilate and Christianize Wisconsin's Indians, had irreparably damaged traditional culture. The context for traditional music disintegrated accordingly, and with it the need for making traditional instruments. At the same time, however, white attacks on indigenous cultures fostered numerous pan-Indian movements, eclectic blends of diverse traditions that stressed the commonality of Indian peoples and the necessity of preserving their identity in opposition to larger American culture.

The Grass Dance was one such movement. Originating on the Great Plains, but spreading by the 1880s to Wisconsin's Ojibwa, Winnebago, Menominee, and Potowatomi, the Grass Dance spawned the Drum Dance Society, a new repertoire of Plains-influenced songs, and the construction of large drums around which a number of players and singers might sit.

Regarded as a "grandfather," a sacred spirit, the dance drum became the focus of a new ceremonialism among many of Wisconsin's native peoples.

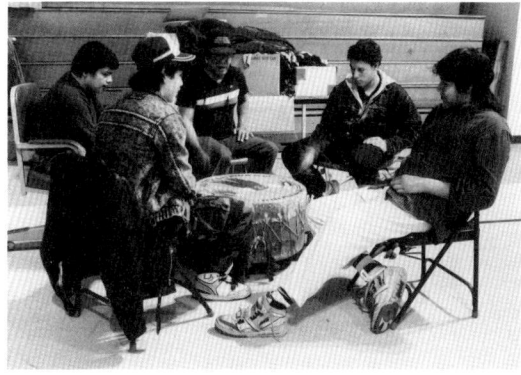

Joseph Ackley, center, and members of the TRAILS youth group he directs play the drum Ackley built for their use.

The contemporary Midwestern powwow, also centered around the big drum, emerged in turn early in the twentieth century, incorporating secularized elements of the Drum Dance movement. Today's singers and players of the dance drum, called "Drums" themselves, travel in warm weather on a powwow circuit throughout the Upper Midwest, performing a body of intertribally known songs for social dancers. Some of them play the factory-made brass drums of marching bands, but many rely on instruments constructed by men like Joseph Ackley.

Indeed the demand for homemade drums is paralleled by a renewed interest in other musical performances on the powwow circuit. Hand drums and medicine games have made a comeback. Meanwhile the revival of the courting flute in pan-Indian circles by commercially recorded players like Kevin Locke, a Sioux, and R. Carlos Nakai, a Navajo, has contributed to a resurgence of interest at Upper Midwestern powwows where Menominee Louis Webster trades his flutes for ribbon shirts, leggings, and moccasins.

EUROPEANS

While Wisconsin's native peoples lacked string instruments, European settlers brought them in abundance. The fiddle—important in folk music throughout Europe by the eighteenth century—was the primary traditional instrument made and played in nineteenth century Wisconsin. French, French-Indians, Yankees, Irish, Belgians, Germans, Slavs, and Scandinavians each fiddled out some combination of jigs, reels, hornpipes, polkas, waltzes, schottisches, krakowiaks, mazurkas, hambos, and numerous other dance forms for doings in homes, barns, community halls, taverns, and outdoor boweries.

Fiddles were especially popular in the lumber camps where jacks of all backgrounds mingled and were often expected, during long winters away from home, to contribute to a weekend's entertainment. Ray Calkins, who went into the woods with his dad about 1905, working as a cookee, then a swamper, recalls a cedar camp north of Ladysmith where there were fiddlers and fiddle-makers aplenty. "A lot of the

Fiddlers seated with other lumberjacks in the bunkhouse of Ole Emerson's logging camp near Cable, Bayfield County, about 1906. (Photo courtesy of the State Historical Society of Wisconsin, Iconographic Collections.)

guys that couldn't buy instruments, they made them: anything that could make some kind of noise." Calkins, like Otto Rindlisbacher, made lumber camp fiddles, guitars, and the Viking cello (a one-stringed bowed instrument based on the Norwegian *psalmodikon*).

By the latter part of the nineteenth century, however, the accordion and the related German concertina had begun to challenge the fiddle's place as the most prevalent instrument in Wisconsin's Eurpean-derived folk music. Whereas the state's first wave of trans-Atlantic immigrants brought fiddles, the second wave—settling the northern cutover and the urban southeast—carried squeezeboxes. With a reedy musical voice more penetrating than the fiddle's, the accordion could be heard amidst a crowd of dancers; and whereas a fiddler typically needed a piano, second fiddle, or guitar for backing, an accordionist could provide melody with the right hand and rhythm with the left.

Accordion and concertina importers and builders established stores in Milwaukee and Chicago, distributing their products throughout the region. By the 1920s the diatonic button accordion was superceded by the piano keyboard accordion in the hands of musicians who entertained at public dances, although it remained common enough among house party players. Together these instruments contributed to the establishment of "Polka," a genre incorporating many couple dance forms in addition to the polka, with many complex ethnic and regional variations. "Polka" extends old world musical forms and even synthesizes them with such "American" musical genres as jazz and country. In the Dairyland's current polka scene, concertinas are especially prominent among Polish and "Dutchman" (German-Bohemian) musicians, while Slo-venians favor four row button accordions with a booming bass sound, and the piano accordion has almost universal appeal.

Norwegians, especially in that part of Wisconsin extending from Dane County west and north through the driftless area, have remained stubborn holdouts for the fiddle—perhaps a legacy of those immigrants from the districts of western and southern Norway where the *hardingfela* or hardanger fiddle was prominent. From the late nineteenth century through the early 1920s Norwegian newcomers included virtuoso players and makers of this ornate and difficult eight-stringed instrument.

Knute and Gunnar Helland, descendants of a noted old country family of fiddle-makers, had set up shop in Chippewa Falls by 1905. Active in the Hardanger Violinist Association of America (established in Ellsworth in 1914), they sponsored competitions *(kappleik)* in Blair, Chippewa Falls, Eau Claire, La Crosse, and Mount Horeb that attracted such stalwarts as Andrea Quisling of Madison, Harold Smedal, the fiddling sheriff of Dane County, and Stoughton tavernkeeper Hans Fykerud. Although the second generation did not adopt the hardanger tradition—with its ties to complex outmoded dance forms like the *springar* and *gangar*, its difficult tunings, and its peculiar resonant sound—Norwegian-Americans and their descendants continued to excel on the four string or "flat" fiddle, investing scores of polkas, waltzes, and schottisches with a distinctive Scandinavian lilt. (Martin 1980: 11) And in the 1970s, classically trained violinists with Scandinavian roots or interests began a revival that led to the formation of the Hardanger Fiddle Association of America in 1983.

While conventional fiddles and accordions were pan-European instruments easily adaptable to life in Wisconsin,

America's most European state, other stringed imports as esoteric as the hardanger fiddle have also managed to survive. Wisconsin's Serbians and Croatians, and even some Slovenians, established tamburitza orchestras in places like Sanborn, Hurley, Eagle River, Willard, Sheboygan, and Milwaukee. Built around a family of lute-like stringed instruments—including the *prim, brac, bugarija,* and *berdo*—these groups played *kolos* and other Balkan line dances for weddings and community gatherings. By the late 1930s, with the decline of the immigrant generation, tamburitza groups faded in rural Yugoslav settlements, but Serbians and Croatians in urban southeastern Wisconsin had sufficient numbers to foster the establishment of an active scene with four piece "combos" entertaining in taverns and at picnics, and larger "junior" tamburitza groups under the schooling of such master players as Charles Elias of Racine.

Tamburitza music in Wisconsin has also benefitted from the national visibility of Pittsburgh's Duquesne University Tamburitzans, a touring ensemble specializing in choreographed presentations of eastern European music, song, and dance. Until their recent demise, the "Tammies" not only toured Wisconsin, but held an annual summer camp at Douglas County's Lake Nebagamon. In addition, members of junior tamburitza groups in industrial Midwestern cities like Milwaukee and Chicago often "graduated" to play at Duquesne, then returned home to form their own combos.

NEWCOMERS

The post World War II era in particular has seen an influx of newcomers seeking work in urban Wisconsin: Europeans, Hispanics from the American Southwest, Mexico, and Puerto Rico, sourthern-born African Americans, and Southeast Asians. Often settling in neighborhoods, they have established social and cultural institutions that include traditional musical performances and demand specialized instruments.

Consumer hunger for exotic cuisine has aided the expansion of Greek restaurants throughout urban America. Their atmosphere is typically enhanced through recordings, and sometimes live performances, of bouzouki music. A long-necked lute, the bouzouki was associated early in this century with *rebetiko,* the musical expression of a former peasant underclass adrift and oppressed in urban Greece. By the late 1940s, however, the bouzouki had merged with the popular music of a growing middle class and had taken on national associations. For the entrepreneurial Greeks in cities like Madison, Sheboygan, and Milwaukee, live bouzouki music has become requisite at ethnic celebrations that often complement local players with musicians from Chicago.

The Latvian *kokle* has a much greater longevity. Archeological evidence suggests that the *kokle,* a sort of plucked zither common in the Baltics, may be as old as the thirteenth century. Nearly extinct in the nineteenth century, a period when folklorists began collecting Latvian folksongs, the instrument has been revived steadily. Since the 1960s Latvian-American refugees from Soviet occupation, many of them intellectuals and professionals, have organized *kokle* ensembles among their offspring who rely on written notes to accompany choral renditions of folksongs. Beyond performing at public concerts locally, *kokle* players from the greater Milwaukee area congregate at national festivals held annually since 1965.

While Latvian-Americans have classicized their ancient folk music and placed it within the context of recent secular events, Milwaukee's Puerto Rican community of factory and service workers sustain their informally acquired *jibaro* music in keeping with a sacred calendar. The music of Spanish-Indian plantation workers from the rural interior of Puerto Rico, *jibaro* music typically features a guitar, one or two *cuatros*, a scraped notched gourd or *guiro*, and perhaps a double-headed drum or a pair of maracas. Favoring couple dance forms, *jibaro* music also relies on solo singers improvising *decimas* (a ten line Spanish verse form found throughout the Caribbean and Latin America) concerning the homeland, love, or religious subjects.

The latter are celebrated especially during *parrandas* ("carolling parties") that extend from early November through mid-January in Puerto Rico, but are generally shortened in Milwaukee to coincide with the mainland Christmas season: from Thanksgiving until *el dia de Reyes* ("Three Kings Day") or the Epiphany. During this period Miguel Cruz, *jibaro* musician and *cuatro* builder, joins with fellow musicians to travel from house to house singing a standard song of greeting on the doorstep, then improvising *decimas* once inside.

African-Americans boast the most vigorous and varied musical culture of any twentieth century newcomers to Wisconsin. Migrating from the southern Mississippi Valley, sometimes by way of Chicago, they have brought blues, rhythm and blues, and gospel sounds, each with numerous substylistic variations, to Milwaukee, Madison, Racine, Kenosha, Beloit, and Janesville. The most stunning African-American traditional instrument is arguably the human voice, full of melismatic grandeur, ranging tonally from bass growls to falsetto whoops, cast in hypnotic call-and-response patterns. Perhaps because African-Americans have participated in American popular music for so long and to such a degree, they have both absorbed and influenced instruments available today through any music store. But they have also generated new musical instruments through a remarkable transformation of pre-existing technology.

The "Hip Hop" subculture that flowered in New York City in the late 1970s and quickly spread throughout urban African-America involved the stylized signatures of graffiti "writing," the fluid athleticism of "break dancing," and the verbal and musical artistry of "rap." The latter featured rhymed narrative commentaries on the urban scene, combined with the clever manipulation of boomboxes and turntables. Using pre-recorded tapes, while "mixing," "cutting," "backspinning," and "scratching" records, youthful Hip Hop DJs in contemporary urban Milwaukee "improve" commercial recordings by combining, repeating, reversing,and agitating grooves to create a new lyrical and rhythmic statement.

The extent to which the Hmong, among Wisconsin's most recent newcomers, will be able to adapt their musical culture to new surroundings remains to be seen. A mountain people from northern Laos, the Hmong were allied with the United States during the Viet Nam war and, in the wake of that conflict, were driven by the Pathet Lao to refugee camps in Thailand. Those arriving in Wisconsin have settled in extended family groups in such medium-sized cities as Eau Claire, La Crosse, Madison, Menomonie, Sheboygan, and Wausau. Immigrant parents have stressed the importance of their children's education and "Americanization," but they have also tried to preserve elements of their culture, including music.

The Hmong mouth organ or *qeej* continues to be used both at funerals, where melodies guide the deceased to the spirit world, and at New Year's festivities, where young men combine *qeej*-playing with martial arts. The two-stringed violin (*nkauj nrog ncas*) and fipple flute (*lub raj pum liv*) of the sort made and played by Wang Chou Vang of Menomonie have

Wang Chou Vang fingers a Hmong flute which he crafted from bamboo.

undergone changes in use. In the old country, Vang and young men like him relied on these instruments for courting.

> When you want to see a girlfriend, they never go out with you. They stay in the house. You stay on the outside. You cannot get in the house and stay with them. Their mother and father don't like it...Then you have to have the flute and violin to play...to tell the people that you are a good person, that you just want to go looking for a girlfriend.

Since the Hmong language is a total one, in which the meaning of syllables depends upon their intonation, it was possible for Vang to replicate monosyllables and tones through instruments—to speak through music.

During wartime he played the violin and flute when entering a village to signal his benign intentions. Nowadays, Vang has forgotten the songs he once improvised back home. Instead his flute tells us: "I left my mother and father behind, and I'm lonely in this country and nobody helps."

SYMBOLS

Despite his distress, Wang Chou Vang continues to make instruments, valiantly finding substitutes for the bamboo

resonators of his violins and covering them with the tanned hides of deer and raccoon he now hunts. He wonders if his children will ever play them, and hopes that they will at least consider instruments important reminders of their cultural heritage, of the richness, mystery, and integrity of the world they have lost. Nor is Vang alone in his wonderings and his hopes. Wisconsin's makers of traditional instruments all recognize that their creations have a symbolic importance that extends well beyond the formal properties of objects and the musical genres for which they are intended.

For many, the instruments are symbolic indicators of their own existence and artistry. Ray Polarski has made fiddles for each of his children as keepsakes. "I'm going to keep making them as long as I can. The Lord has blessed me with a steady hand." Evidence of George Karpek's steady hand is abundantly clear on the shelves of his old store where gorgeously inlaid accordions, restored and maintained by his descendants, glitter on shelves for show but not for sale.

Karpek's desire that his accordions would become personal symbols, not only for himself but for others, is reflected by his practice of inscribing each with the Karpek name and the name of its owner. Such customization went further in the case of Concertina Millie Kaminski, a noted figure in Milwaukee's old time music scene. Karpek serviced Millie's concertina: affixing a name plate, repairing a wire or a key. Once she told him about locking her keys in the car and lacking the change to call her husband. Karpek surprised her with a silver dime glued on the concertina as a reminder against future absent-mindedness. But today the coin reminds Millie of days past when Milwaukee's squeezebox players would gather to jam at Karpek's on Thurday nights: "It was just like a George Karpek Club."

The elusive past that traditional instruments conjure is often viewed with nostalgia as a "golden age." The walls of Otto Rindlisbacher's Buckhorn Tavern in Rice Lake were festooned with arcane instruments he had made, repaired, or collected. If urged or in the right mood, he would bring them down—*langeleiks*, cigar box guitars, hardanger fiddles—reveal their pedigrees, and coax them into life. Then they would go back on the walls, "conversation pieces" to spark the old and the curious.

On a few occasions instruments have even symbolized a non-existent past. When the Wisconsin Lumberjacks played for the National Folk Festival in 1938, organizer Sarah Gertrude Knott wondered about a strange instrument: a pitchfork, with a wooden soundbox over which a single string stretched, topped off with a carved lion's head. Otto Rindlisbacher and Ray Calkins informed her that it had no real name, but was something a Norwegian lumberjack had cobbled up after a *psalmodikon*, a simple bowed instrument used by Scandinavian Lutherans to accompany hymnsinging. The lion's head was a whimsical reference to the ornate hardanger fiddle. Dissatisfied, Knott dubbed it the Viking Cello, a sobriquet that oddly combined the romance of pagan brigandage with the respectability of a string quartet, neither of which had much to do with Norwegian Lutherans in the Wisconsin pinery.

While Knott's revision of the past was that of an outsider attempting to present north woods music before a national audience as a quaint and curious slice of living regional Americana, numerous ethnic groups have used musical instruments as a means of revitalizing, even reinventing, their own cultures. The rise of nation states in nineteenth century Europe was marked by a concomitant celebration of national culture, and

Framed Latvian *kokle* in the living room of Konstantins Dravnieks, Thiensville.

folk culture was commonly regarded as the essence of national culture. Particular folk tales, songs, customs, dances, and musical instruments were elevated as priceless possessions of the people. And particular solo instruments considered especially significant for a given nation were newly constructed in standard, bass, and tenor forms. Folk orchestras of Russian balalaikas, Italian mandolins, Serbo-Croatian tamburitzas, Finnish *kanteles*, and Latvian *kokles* prospered. Such use of selective aspects of folk culture to represent a people not only provided central images for the declaration of uniqueness, but also offered rallying points in the face of external threats.

A tamburitza by Nick Vukusich is among the raffle prizes at a benefit in the Milwaukee Croatian community.

In contemporary Wisconsin, musical instruments have often become important public symbols of ethnic identity. The grand prize at Croatian community fundraisers in Milwaukee has regularly been a tamburitza crafted by Nick Vukusich. Young Latvian-Americans unable to speak the language use their ability to play the *kokle* as an expression of kinship both with their emigre parents and with those under imperialist domination in the old country. Meanwhile young Ojibwas under Joseph Ackley's tutelage learn to treat with respect the drum that connects them with their elders.

And yet Wisconsin's traditional instrument-makers know that the cultural symbolism of their art means little if the culture itself is not protected. Scornful of instruments perpetually hung mute on walls, many instrument-makers refuse to sell a flute, a drum, a fiddle that will not be played. Many might paraphrase Joseph Ackley's Ojibwa dictum: "The old people say, 'When the drum stops, our race will be extinct.'"

James P. Leary
Wisconsin Folk Museum
Mount Horeb

SOURCES

Allen, Ray, and Nancy Groce. 1988. *Folk and Traditional Music in New York State*, special issue of *New York Folklore* 14:3-4.

Catlin, Amy. 1985. "The Hmong and Their Music...A Critique of Pure Speech." In *Hmong Art, Tradition and Change.* Sheboygan, Wisconsin: John Michael Kohler Arts Center.

Densmore, Frances. 1910 & 1913. *Chippewa Music.* Washington, D.C.: Smithsonian Institution, Bureau of American Ethnology.

Geiser, Brigitte. 1976. *Musical Instruments in the Swiss Folk Tradition.* Zurcich: Pro Helvetia.

Leary, James P. 1984. "Old Time Music in Northern Wisconsin." *American Music* 2:1, 71-88.

———. 1987. *The Wisconsin Patchwork: The Field Recordings of Helene Stratman-Thomas.* Madison: Department of Continuing Education in the Arts, University of Wisconsin.

March, Richard. 1983. "The Tamburitza Tradition." Bloomington: Ph.D dissertation in Folklore, Indiana University.

Martin, Philip. 1976. "Ed Johnson, Heavenly Sounds from the Devil's Instrument." *Wisconsin Trails.* 17:4, 10-11.

———. 1979. "The Hardanger Fiddle in Wisconsin." *Ocooch Mountain News* 5:8, 10-11.

———. 1980. "Hardanger Fiddlers." *Ocooch Mountain News.* 6:1, 10-11.

Niles, Christina. 1978. "The Revival of the Latvian Kokle in America." *Selected Reports in Ethnomusicology* 3:1, 211-239.

Russell, Olga Karpek. 1975. *This Is Our Lives.* Privately printed.

Sadie, Stanley, ed. 1984. *The New Grove Dictionary of Musical Instruments.* London & NYC: Macmillan Press, Ltd.

Starr, Mary Agnes. 1960s. Field recording of the Wisconsin Lumberjacks for the State Historical Society of Wisconsin, Sound Recordings Division.

Vennum, Thomas, Jr. 1982. *The Ojibwa Dance Drum, Its History and Construction.* Washington, D.C.: Smithsonian Institution Press, Smithsonian Folklife Studies, Number 2.

PAST MASTERS

KARPEK ACCORDIONS:
A SOUTH SIDE INSTITUTION

ANDREW AND GEORGE KARPEK

Milwaukee, Wisconsin

Piano and Button Accordions, Concertinas

The Karpek Accordion Manufacturing Company, located on Sixteenth Street on Milwaukee's South Side.

From the 1920s through the early 1950s, the Karpek Accordion Manufacturing Company was the hub of accordion music on Milwaukee's South Side. In the company's workshops, a staff of skilled craftsmen constructed some of the country's finest piano and button accordions and concertinas. In Karpek's basement studios, five full-time accordion teachers offered lessons to eager students. And in the Karpek showroom, squeezebox players from throughout Milwaukee gathered on Thursday afternoons to try out new instruments, talk, and play music.

The Karpek Accordion Manufacturing Company began in 1915 when Andrew Karpek, a Russian immigrant, decided to use the experience he had gained in the old country to open a shop at 820 South 16th Street. An extraordinary craftsman and an innovator who

was the first to install an amplifier in an accordion, Andrew ran the family business until his death in 1942. He was succeeded by his son George who had worked alongside his father "ever since I could handle a tool." Like his father, George ran the business until he passed away in 1988. His wife Grace and their daughter Georjann now carry on with the help of several part-time repair workers, maintaining the showroom and workshop at the same address they have had for seventy-five years.

For three decades, from the twenties through the forties, Andrew and George Karpek hand-crafted a stunning array of piano accordions for such greats as Lawrence Welk and Frankie Yankovic. Multi-colored, inlaid with pearl and rhinestones, adorned with ornate open-work grilles, and bearing the Karpek name, their instruments set the standard for a thriving industry.

The rock and roll boom of the 1950s, however, brought an abrupt end to the efflorescence of accordion-making and accordion music in this country. The guitar-based rock of Chuck Berry and Elvis Presley captured the ear of America's youth, and the accordion business began a steady decline. As a result, George Karpek was forced to cut back his staff and to begin devoting most of his time and energies to repair work and the resale of used instruments. Once the lively center of a vital business and musical tradition, the Karpek Accordion Manufacturing Company stands now as one of only three Milwaukee area music stores still selling the instruments.

The Milwaukee Accordion School. (Photo from "A Catalogue of Karpek Accordions," 1935, courtesy of Grace Karpek, Milwaukee.)

Early Karpek accordions,
carefully restored to
their original condition,
still line the shelves of
the Sixteenth Street
showroom today.

EDWIN JOHNSON
Hayward, Wisconsin

Fiddles, Nyckelharpor

"The difference between playing by ear and reading notes is like the difference between reading a book and telling a story."

As a boy in the parish of Rattvik in Sweden's Dalarna province, Edwin Johnson would go to weddings and listen to the fiddlers, learning their tunes by ear. He made his first fiddle at the age of 11, and he brought his second fiddle with him when he immigrated to Minneapolis at the age of 19 in 1924. When Johnson received Wisconsin's first Governor's Heritage Award in 1984 for his lifelong efforts at preserving Swedish traditional music, he played a fiddle made from portions of the old spruce woodbox he had filled so frequently at his grandmother's home in Rattvik.

Edwin Johnson's later instruments might not have incorporated such symbolic materials, but they reflected their maker's expert craftsmanship and extraordinary knowledge of early Swedish music. Johnson's fiddles were often constructed using a special technique of lamination which yielded alternating light and dark stripes or rings in the carved tops of the instruments. He also built several *nyckelharpor*, large, lap-sized fiddles with mechanical wooden keys, believed to have originated during the Medieval period.

An accomplished musician as well as a skilled instrument-maker, Edwin Johnson never forgot the tunes of his boyhood. Like his fiddle, he brought the tunes with him to the United States and he taught them to his children. Johnson's son Bruce began fiddling at the age of 10 and his daughter Nancy mastered the autoharp. With their father, and more recently with Nancy's son Paul, they have performed widely as the American Swedish Spelman's Trio, preserving and passing along some 200 old tunes and the old-fashioned chorded accompaniment which long ago faded or disappeared in Edwin's native Sweden.

Following his immigration to Minneapolis, Johnson met and married his wife Elsie. He worked as a plasterer for most of his life, though he did serve the defense effort as a welder during World War II. Through the years, the Johnson family vacationed frequently in the area of Hayward, Wisconsin. Drawn by the muskie fishing he always enjoyed on their vacations, Edwin and Elsie moved to Hayward following his retirement in 1968. Edwin Johnson passed away in 1984.

Edwin Johnson playing
the *nyckelharpa,* a keyed
Swedish fiddle, during
the early 1980s.

COURTING FLUTES AMONG
WISCONSIN'S WOODLAND INDIANS

Historical Background

Although drums of various sizes and functions played a central role in the lives of Wisconsin's Woodland Indians, melodic instruments were less common. Among the Ojibwa, the wooden courting flute *(bibigwan)* was the only example of this type. Similar flutes were made and used for similar purposes by other Wisconsin tribes, including the Winnebago and Menominee, and at one time these instruments enjoyed widespread distribution among Native Americans generally.

The courting flutes, or lover's flutes, of Wisconsin's Woodland peoples resembled recorders. They were end-blown duct flutes, the tones of which were regulated by movable blocks tied to them. Among the Ojibwa, the flutes ranged in length from fifteen to twenty inches, although smaller versions were made for children to use as toys. Most Ojibwa flutes had five or six holes, and the melodies played upon them were frequently love songs performed by a young man courting a girl's affection. The tradition of flute playing and its social use seems to have persisted longer among other Wisconsin Woodland tribes than among the Ojibwa. However, the practice all but disappeared until a recent revival of interest in association with the contemporary powwow movement.

Frank James playing the Ojibwa courting flute at Lac Court Oreilles about 1941. (Photo by Robert Ritzenthaler, courtesy of the Milwaukee Public Museum, Department of Anthropology, neg. no. 5762.)

WISCONSIN INDIAN MUSICAL INSTRUMENTS

JAMES RAZER
Tony, Wisconsin

Hand Drums, Rattles and Jingles

James Razer was born in Minnesota in 1928. He is an enrolled member of the Fond du Lac Band of Ojibwa, a band occupying lands just south of Duluth and near the Wisconsin border. At the age of five months, Razer was placed in a school operated by the State of Minnesota. The only Indian in the school, Razer was not allowed to communicate with his relatives. He was cut off from his cultural heritage and made to feel ashamed of it. The negative stereotype of Indians which Razer confronted during his fourteen years in the state school prompted him to undertake a lifelong search for his own roots. It also led him to attempt to prove that "the old stuff could be beautiful."

Razer began reading and researching his background. He learned from Frances Densmore's *Chippewa Customs* that his great-grandmother, Mrs. Frank Razer of the White Earth Reservation, was known for her beadwork and crafts. Eventually, Razer began talking to tribal elders. He became involved in dancing in an effort to recover a sense of his cultural past, and he was an active participant in powwows for many years. In the early 1980s, after raising a family and retiring from work as a journeyman electrician for the State of Wisconsin, Razer began presenting public programs to explain and interpret Ojibwa dance, crafts and dress.

At about the age of thirty-five, in conjunction with his dancing, Razer started fashioning traditional garments and accoutrements of the type made by Woodland peoples prior to contact with whites. Among the articles Razer creates are a number of musical instruments. These include deer toe jingles to adorn buckskin dance leggings, turtle shell rattles used for curing ceremonies, warrior's whistles made from the wingbone of an eagle, small hand drums to accompany moccasin games, and larger social drums fashioned from hollowed-out cottonwood stumps.

Although James Razer does not consider himself an artist and has turned to historical reconstruction to learn certain of his crafts, he continues a tradition of Ojibwa instrument-making which contributes to the maintenance of the tribe's material culture and helps to express his Indian identity.

James Razer wears
Ojibwa dance regalia
which he has fashioned
entirely of natural
materials. Deer toe
jingles encircle the tops
of his leggings. (Photo
courtesy of James Razer.)

LOUIS WEBSTER
Neopit, Wisconsin

End-blown Flutes

While attending classes at the University of Wisconsin-Milwaukee in the early 1970s, Louis Webster was introduced to a variety of Native American musical instruments by an ethnomusicology instructor. Among these was a Sioux flute. A talented musician of mixed Woodland heritage, Webster was fascinated by the flute and decided to make one for himself. The first attempt at instrument making proved highly successful, and Webster began working flute tunes into his musical compositions. These he performed while traveling the emerging Midwestern powwow circuit. Webster soon encountered other flute players, young and old, at the powwows he attended, and he began making more instruments for barter and sale to this clientele and to other interested parties. Through the efforts of Louis Webster over the past fifteen to twenty years, the Woodland flute has experienced a marked revival, regaining something of the popularity and cultural significance it enjoyed early in this century.

Born in Green Bay in 1949 of Menominee, Oneida, Ojibwa, Stockbridge, Munsee and Potowatomi ancestry, Louis Webster was adopted by his grandparents at the age of eight months. He was raised on the Menominee Reservation at Neopit. In the early 1960s, Webster began playing rock music and progressed rapidly through various styles. During the late 1960s, he roamed throughout the country, spending several years in San Francisco. By the time of his return to Wisconsin around 1970, the highly political American Indian Movement had grown strong, and Webster became actively involved in Indian politics and culture. He performed in an Indian musical and theatrical group, and he led "Little Big Band," an aggregation that combined blues, country and bluegrass with Indian drum rhythms, singing in vocables, and Webster's flute playing.

While Webster sometimes fashions his flutes from local cedar, he prefers redwood for its grain, looks, workability and durability. Webster buys his redwood from the lumberyard in blocks, then gouges and chisels out the interior of the two halves of the flute's body. Once completed, these are glued together. The thickness of the wood and the wooden reed, bound to the top of the flute with a "saddle," determine the sound of the instrument. Typically, Webster's flutes have six or seven holes and play a seven tone scale.

Although Webster makes some simple, unadorned flutes, many of his instruments are quite ornate, featuring saddles in the form of ducks or bears and mouths bearing the images of birds and beasts. These are not traditional Menominee designs; some, in fact, resemble Sioux patterns. However, Menominee clan animals are often incorporated into Webster's flutes, and dreams provide inspiration for some of his design motifs.

A pair of Webster woodpecker flutes displayed on a gift shop sales counter.

Two Webster
flutes rest amid
the tools on his
workbench.

JOSEPH ACKLEY

Lac du Flambeau, Wisconsin

Social Drums

"The old people say, 'When the drum stops, our race will be extinct.'"

Joseph Ackley was born in 1940 at L' Anse, Michigan, and raised in Wisconsin on the Bad River Reservation. His grandfather, Willard Ackley, was the last chief of the Mole Lake Band of Ojibwa; his father, Charles Ackley, passed along much of his specialized knowledge of Ojibwa culture to him. Like both his father and grandfather, Joe Ackley is a traditional person with regard to religion and he is a drum-maker.

The drums which Joe Ackley makes are not sacred drums intended for religious ceremonies. Rather, they are social drums for use in intertribal powwows. Despite their secular use, however, Ackley treats his drums in a fashion which stresses their symbolic importance in Ojibwa life. He makes a drum only when one is needed.

Once constructed, the drum is the focus of a feast for those who will play it and sing over it. Thereafter, the drum belongs to those people and they must care for it with respect: storing it with its head at right angles to the floor, transporting it wrapped in blankets, and guarding against its handling by those to whom it does not belong.

Though Joe Ackley treats his drums with the reverence and respect shown instruments of old, he employs somewhat more contemporary methods in their construction. Unlike his ancestors, Ackley does not hollow out a log for the body of his drum. Instead, he uses a wooden barrel, the conventional Woodland drum body for about the last fifty years. The interior of the barrel is braced with sticks and a small hole is made in the drum's wall so that air may escape when the drum is played. The top and bottom heads of the drum are typically of rawhide from a deer Ackley has hunted. Holes are made in the edges of the drumheads for laces which tie top and bottom together. Once taken on by a group of players and singers, generically termed a "drum," the top head is painted with emblems of the group. Fiberglass or wooden sticks with padded ends and sometimes adorned with feathers or beadwork are used to play the instrument.

As a young man, Ackley danced to the drum as others played. Later he began to play and sing, eventually becoming a lead singer with a preference for the low-pitched Ojibwa style. He currently belongs to two drum groups and cares for the instruments he has made for each. One group is his own Woodland Woodtick Singers. The other is the TRAILS drum of Lac du Flambeau. TRAILS is a youth program run by Ackley which emphasizes the importance of traditional values and points out the damaging effects of drugs and alcohol. One of the group's principal activities is playing, singing over, and caring for its drum.

Drums belonging to the
Woodland Wood Ticks
and the TRAILS youth
group are stored at right
angles to the floor in
Joseph Ackley's home.

OTTO RINDLISBACHER
Rice Lake, Wisconsin

Fiddles and Lumberjack Instruments

Otto Rindlisbacher
playing the button
accordion. (Photo
courtesy of the State
Historical Society of
Wisconsin, Iconographic
Collections.)

Otto Rindlisbacher was born in Athens, Wisconsin in 1895 of
Swiss-German heritage. He moved to Rice Lake with his family
as a young man. In 1920, after working briefly in the woods and
sawmills, he opened a billiard parlor and cafe known as The Buckhorn.
Following the repeal of prohibition, The Buckhorn became a tavern.
Rindlisbacher operated the establishment until shortly before his
death in 1975. In the course of its long history, The Buckhorn became
the repository of "The World's Largest Collection of 'Odd Lumberjack Musical Instruments.'" At the same time, Otto Rindlisbacher
came to be perhaps the foremost figure in the history of traditional
music in Wisconsin.

Rindlisbacher learned to play *laendlers* and a variety of Swiss
dance tunes on button and piano accordion at an early age. As a
teen, he toured with Thorstein Skarning, a Norwegian bandleader
from Minneapolis who performed widely throughout northwestern
Wisconsin. Around 1920 Rindlisbacher recorded 78 rpm discs of Swiss
music with Karl Hoppe. During the early 1920s, he performed
Hawaiian music over the radio as a member of a band which also
included his wife Iva. And in 1926 and 1927, Rindlisbacher organized
old time fiddle contests.

Rindlisbacher assisted ballad scholar Franz Rickaby in the
collection of Wisconsin lumberjack songs, and this contact may have
led to an invitation from the National Folk Festival to bring a
lumberjack group to Chicago for its 1937 event. Rindlisbacher formed
"The Wisconsin Lumberjacks," and the group performed at the
National several times during the late 1930s. Later, he passed the
band along to another of its original members, Ray Calkins, who
kept it going for over twenty years. In 1940 and 1946, Otto Rindlisbacher
was recorded by Helene Stratman-Thomas for the Library of
Congress, and some of his lumberjack tunes were issued on a Library
recording. Some of Rindlisbacher's other tunes, mainly Swiss
laendlers and Norwegian hardanger fiddle pieces, were later issued
on the Wisconsin Patchwork series of radio programs and cassettes.

In addition to his prowess as a musician, Rindlisbacher was
highly regarded for his skill as an instrument-maker. He crafted both
conventional or "flat" fiddles and elaborate Norwegian hardanger
fiddles. He also demonstrated his considerable talents by creating
miniature fiddles, some of them small enough to fit into a ring.
Rindlisbacher also made a number of the lumberjack instruments
common to northwestern Wisconsin. These included cigar box fiddles
and guitars, "bull" fiddles or gut-bucket basses, and "Viking Cellos."

Promotional postcard
showing Otto
Rindlisbacher playing
hardanger fiddle before
the Buckhorn Tavern's
extensive collection of
musical instruments.
(Photo courtesy of
James P. Leary.)

RAY CALKINS
Chetek, Wisconsin

Cigar Box Fiddles and Guitars, Lumberjack Instruments

Ray Calkins playing a "Viking cello" of his own construction. (Photo courtesy of James P. Leary.)

The songs and stories of Wisconsin's lumber camps captured Ray Calkins fancy as a young boy, and he has spent many of his ninety-five years sharing these occupational and regional tunes and tales with others throughout the state and the country.

Ray Calkins was born in 1894, seven miles east of Chetek in Barron County, Wisconsin. Both his father and grandfather worked in the lumber camps in the northwestern part of the state. At the age of eleven or twelve, Ray followed them into the woods, working first as a cookee and later as a swamper in the camps where his father was employed.

Calkins began playing drums as a member of a school band in Chetek. He also played the old pump organ, chording for dances. In addition, Ray Calkins learned to play violin, banjo, bass fiddle, mandolin, piano and button accordion. While working in the lumber camps, Ray played a great deal of music and heard many fine fiddlers.

In 1937, Otto Rindlisbacher of Rice Lake was contacted by Sarah Gertrude Knott and invited to bring a lumberjack band to the National Folk Festival in Chicago. Ray Calkins had often played for dances with Rindlisbacher, and he was asked to join the band. The group, "The Wisconsin Lumberjacks," included Otto Rindlisbacher and his wife Iva, Calkins, Frank Uchytil from Haugen, and Buck Plante, a Frenchman from Ladysmith. The group "went over like a top" in Chicago and later played in Washington, D.C. Following these early appearances, Otto Rindlisbacher asked Calkins to take over the group. He agreed to do so, and under his direction, "The Wisconsin Lumberjacks" performed for the National Folk Festival well into the 1960s.

Dressed in wool pants, wool shirts and felt or stocking caps, "The Wisconsin Lumberjacks" played various homemade instruments: cigar box fiddles, cigar box guitars or "Paul Bunyan harps," the garbage can bass or "bangola," and the "Viking Cello," a one-stringed instrument made from a pitchfork and patterned after the Scandinavian *psalmodikon*. While Otto Rindlisbacher originally made all of these instruments, Ray Calkins later came to make the entire range himself. Their simple construction harks back to the homemade fiddles and guitars Calkins knew in the Wisconsin lumber camps of his boyhood.

Cookees and fiddlers in the dining hall of August Mason's lumber camp in Barron County, 1902. (Photo courtesy of the State Historical Society of Wisconsin, Iconographic Collections.)

The Wisconsin
Lumberjacks—with Ray
Calkins on the cigar box
guitar at left—per-
forming at the National
Folk Festival in
Covington, Kentucky in
1963. (Photo courtesy of
the Rusk County Histori-
cal Society, Ladysmith.)

RAY POLARSKI
Three Lakes, Wisconsin

Fiddles

Ray Polarski demonstrates his "hoe down" style of fiddling, holding the instrument against his chest instead of under his chin.

"The good Lord has blessed me with a steady hand."

The music of Wisconsin's north woods has always been an important part of Ray Polarski's life. Born on a farm near Three Lakes in 1915, Polarski heard many local favorites from his father at an early age. A good button accordion and concertina player, Joe Polarski often entertained at house parties, dances and weddings. In addition, Ray Polarski listened to the fiddle tunes of Wesley Warden, a French-Canadian neighbor who played together with an accordionist.

Polarski also enjoyed an early introduction to one of the area's most prominent crafts, woodworking. As a boy, he was always "handy with a jack knife." He carved cedar fans, whistles, and even a wooden fiddle. He also saw local lumberjacks—especially Finns— carve wooden chains, balls-in-cages, and canes with wooden dice in the handles.

At the age of thirteen, Polarski repaired a fiddle for his neighbor Wesley Warden. In return, Warden taught him to play "Little Brown Jug." Polarski determined then and there to make a fiddle of his own. His first instruments were rather rough, like cigar box fiddles, but Ray Polarski had his start as an instrument-maker and musician.

Since the late 1930s, Polarski has made about 50 violins. True to his background, he has frequently used local woods—maple, walnut, pine, balsam and cedar—for his instruments. Polarski does, however, use imported woods for bridges, pegs, and other parts. Occasionally, he will also utilize straight-grained Sitka spruce for his fiddle tops. Beautifully made and well varnished, Polarski's instruments are appealing to the eye. Light in weight and having both good action and fine tone, his fiddles are also a delight to the hand and ear.

Ray Polarski has made a fiddle for each of his children and has given others to his siblings. He has also sold some of his instruments, but there is little market for them in northern Wisconsin. Consequently, Polarski has treated his instrument-making as a hobby, relying for his livelihood on farming and carpentry work. While his reputation as a fiddler and fiddle-maker may be limited to family and local seniors with a taste for old time music, Polarski hopes to continue making instruments for a long time. "The good Lord has blessed me with a steady hand," he says. He is also passing along his skills to another Three Lakes man, Scott Brewster.

Ray Polarski works on a fiddle bow.

Polarski's appreciation
for fine wood is reflected
in the beautiful grain
of this fiddle back.

SOUND DESIGN

EPAMINONTAS BOURANTAS
Milwaukee, Wisconsin

Greek Bouzoukis

Just over twenty years ago, Epaminontas Bourantas received a bouzouki as a gift. Raised in Greece and long an active member of the Milwaukee Greek-American community, Bourantas was well acquainted with the pear-shaped instruments and the music they added to seasonal and ceremonial life. Consequently, he was somewhat disappointed when he discovered that the bouzouki he had been given produced several "sour" notes. Rather than simply setting the instrument aside, Bourantas decided to take it apart to see how it was made and to attempt to build an improved version. Since that time, he has striven continuously to build a better bouzouki.

"George" Bourantas came to the task of designing and building bouzoukis well prepared. Not only was he familiar with the instruments and their sound, he was also skilled in mathematics, drafting and tool manipulation as a result of his training and experience in aircraft maintenance and his long career as a machine builder for Allen Bradley. After consulting with a few other instrument-makers in Greece and doing some reading, Bourantas began making blueprints and drawings for the construction of his bouzoukis. He also constructed a set of "jigs" or forms for bending and shaping instrument parts, especially those which compose the base and are simultaneously curved, tapered and beveled. Similarly, Bourantas made or modified a variety of tools to suit his particular purposes.

George Bourantas made his first bouzouki in 1969 and has continued to produce them at a rate of three or four per year. With each instrument, he seeks to achieve "superb sound" and "accurate tone" as well as exceptional beauty. Every bouzouki Bourantas creates is a composite of 1,003 parts, each of which has been fashioned by hand and fits integrally with other elements. He uses only woods that have been aged for at least ten years and varies his selection of rosewood, teak, black walnut and Sitka spruce to achieve the best aural and visual effects. His frets are made of German silver, and the soundboards of his instruments are inlaid with Greek motifs in wood, plastic and mother-of-pearl. Once Bourantas has assembled the various parts of his bouzoukis using several specialized glues, he coats the bodies of the instruments with a layer of egg white to prevent subsequent layers of clear finish from penetrating the wood and deadening the sound. Finally, upon completion, Bourantas has each of his bouzoukis tested for sound by a professional musician.

Because the Greek bouzouki, like the Latvian *kokle* or Croatian tamburitza, is a symbol of ethnic identity and national pride, those who craft and play the instrument enjoy a special status within their communities. Through his exceptional craftsmanship and long commitment to improving the bouzoukis he builds, George Bourantas has earned an even higher level of appreciation from the musicians and other members of his Greek-American community.

Two Bourantas
bouzoukis with inlaid
soundboards and
fingerboards rest on his
basement workbench.

THE BALDONIS OF CASTELFIDARDO:
FOUR GENERATIONS OF ACCORDION - MAKERS

ALFONSO AND IVO BALDONI
Milwaukee, Wisconsin

Piano and Button Accordions, Concertinas

"He learned from me, like I learned from my father as a child."

Alfonso Baldoni checks an accordion at his workbench.

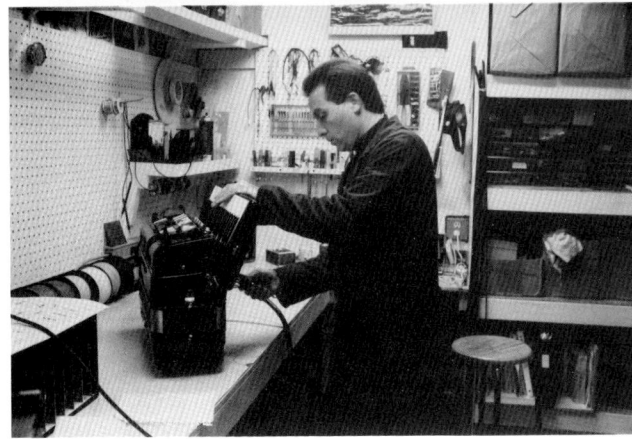

Alfonso's son, Ivo, inspects an accordion in the shop of A. Baldoni Music Service, Milwaukee.

Alfonso and Ivo Baldoni, proprietors of A. Baldoni Music Service in Milwaukee, represent the third and fourth generations of their family actively involved in the manufacture of accordions. Both Alfonso and his son Ivo were born in Castelfidardo, Italy, the city that is to the accordion what Cremona is to the violin. Alfonso's father and grandfather worked as artisans, making components for accordion companies. Alfonso's father was also a noted reed-maker, and his son learned a great deal about building accordions from observing him working at home. At the age of twelve, Alfonso began learning to play the accordion; by fourteen, he had started to tune the instruments. When he was nineteen years old, Alfonso became an apprentice to a major accordion manufacturer, and within four years he had advanced to the position of foreman.

In 1956, Alfonso Baldoni was hired by a Milwaukee firm to supervise its accordion manufacturing operation in the United States. He brought his wife Nancy and young son to Wisconsin and began sixteen years of work as an accordion-maker and plant foreman. During this period, Alfonso set up a basement workshop and took on a variety of repair jobs. He also taught Ivo the art of building and repairing instruments. In 1972, Alfonso quit his job and opened A. Baldoni Music Service in partnership with his son. The family-owned music store has grown steadily, from primarily a service and repair operation to a sales and service facility. Alfonso specializes in accordions, while Ivo concentrates on the restoration, repair and construction of guitars and other stringed instruments.

In partnership with their relatives in Castelfidardo, the Baldonis manufacture their own line of accordions. Working from Alfonso and Ivo's specifications, family members in Italy construct a range of piano accordions, button accordions, and concertinas aimed at various segments of the American market. In addition to a standard piano accordion directed toward the "American Polka" audience, a jazz and chamber model, and a digitally-equipped electronic accordion, the Baldonis build and customize button boxes for Italian, Slovenian, Chicano and Cajun markets. In all their instruments, the Baldoni family stresses quality materials and craftsmanship. The bodies of their accordions are made of solid wood rather than plywood; the soundboards are of Norwegian spruce, not pine; and the reeds are handmade rather than simply hand-finished. The results of the Baldonis' efforts are not lost on their notable and growing clientele. As Ivo states, "It's like manufacturing your standard automobile or a piece of art work. It's like making a Chevrolet or a Mercedes."

The Baldoni showroom
boasts a large selection
of custom accordions,
button accordions,
and guitars.

RON POAST

Black Earth, Wisconsin

Norwegian Hardanger Fiddles

Ron Poast scrapes the top of a hardanger fiddle.

Ron Poast was born in Dodgeville, Wisconsin, in 1940 of Norwegian heritage. He grew up on a farm in the Blue Mounds area of Dane County. Both of Ron's grandfathers were old time fiddlers, playing in "hillbilly" and Norwegian styles. Ron's dad also played music, and he himself took up the guitar. During Ron's youth, musical house parties were a regular occurrence in the Poast family, bringing together neighbors and friends for dancing and socializing.

As a boy, Ron Poast occasionally heard his relatives speak of a peculiar, very ornate, multi-stringed fiddle which they had seen and heard years before. Though they did not know it, the instrument Poast's family referred to was a *hardingfela*, or a hardanger fiddle, the national folk instrument of Norway. While very popular in the Upper Midwest around the turn of the century following the massive influx of Scandinavian immigrants to the region, the hardanger fiddle declined considerably in popularity by the time of World War II. Few people still played the instrument, and even fewer knew how they were made.

It was not until years after first hearing of these unusual instruments that Ron Poast finally encountered a hardanger fiddle, on display in a shop window in Mount Horeb, Wisconsin. By that time, Poast—an inveterate wood and metal worker, classic car restorer, auto mechanic and luthier—had already been building guitars and banjos for C. C. Richelieu in Oregon, Wisconsin. He began immediately to study the making of hardanger fiddles. Poast visited Vesterheim, the Norwegian-American Museum, in Decorah, Iowa, to examine old instruments. He procured an instruction manual from Norway, and he talked to some of the again-growing number of fiddlers playing the instrument. Since the chance encounter with his first hardanger fiddle, Ron Poast has built fifteen of the instruments and has gained a national reputation as one of only five hardanger makers in the country.

Though similar to the conventional, or "flat," fiddle, the hardanger is distinct in ways subtle and apparent. Its wood is thinner and it is somewhat lighter than the conventional violin. The gauge of hardanger strings is also lighter. More obviously, the hardanger fiddle has eight or nine strings: four ride atop the bridge and fingerboard and are bowed, four or five are strung through the bridge and below the fingerboard and resonate. The result is a droning sound, often likened to a Scottish bagpipe. In addition, the conventional fiddle's scroll is replaced on the hardanger by a stylized lion's head, and the "purfling," or inlaid decoration, is supplemented, front and back, by floral "rosing" done in India ink.

The recent resurgence of interest in hardanger fiddle music, coupled with the extraordinary craftsmanship of Wisconsin instrument-makers like Ron Poast, seem to promise a continued life for this Norwegian fiddle which almost disappeared from the Upper Midwest several decades ago.

A stylized lion's
head replaces the
scroll on a Poast
hardanger fiddle.

NICK VUKUSICH

Milwaukee, Wisconsin

Tamburitzas

As a boy in the Croatian community of Ironwood, Michigan, Nick Vukusich heard a great deal of tamburitza music. Like many others of his generation, Vukusich learned to play the instrument and to perform the music which had become something of a national symbol for Croations since the arrival of the first Yugoslav immigrants in the United States in the 1880s. Tamburitza music later became a Vukusich family tradition as well. Nick and his wife Mary Ann, also a tamburitza player, raised three daughters. All of the girls also took up the instrument and learned to play the Croatian folk tunes handed down in their family and the Milwaukee Croatian community.

Nick Vukusich made his first tamburitza just over twenty years ago. Using some of the woodworking skills he had learned as a youngster while summering with his grandfather in Mellen, Wisconsin, Vukusich took apart an old instrument to see how it was constructed, then built a new one using it as a pattern. Over the years, he has crafted more than 25 tamburitzas for members of his family and for musicians in Milwaukee's Croatian-American community. So highly valued is his craftmanship that Vukusich tamburitzas have been coveted prizes in raffles sponsored by Croatian music groups in the area.

A family of pear-shaped, lute-like instruments introduced into the Balkans centuries ago by the Ottoman Turks, tamburitzas vary in size and function. The smallest instruments in the group, the *bisernica* or *prim* and the *brac* are used to play the lead melody. The *bugarija* is used for chords, while the tamburitza cello and bass provide additional accompaniment.

Nick Vukusich builds his tamburitzas in his spare time in a small shop set up in his basement. He begins by steaming two pieces of ¾" rosewood and placing them in a vise-like wooden mold made to match the shape of the instrument's body. The steam-bent rosewood forms the sides of the instrument. Vukusich then glues the neck, with its ebony fretboard, the tailpiece, and the back onto the sides. For the backs of his tamburitzas, Vukusich often uses bird's eye maple from his brother's Michigan farm or curly maple cut by his grandfather in Mellen some 60 years ago. Cedar support braces are inserted while the instrument is still in the mold. Vukusich then removes the tamburitza from the form and glues the top, which has also been braced, into place. For the tops of his instruments, Vukusich uses spruce, inlaid with rosewood, which is in turn inlaid with tiny flower-shaped pieces of mother-of-pearl.

A completed Vukusich
tamburitza stands before
the partially constructed
bodies of two other
instruments in his base-
ment workshop.

KONSTANTINS DRAVNIEKS
Thiensville, Wisconsin

Latvian Kokles

Konstantins Dravnieks was born of Latvian parents in Petrograd on May 21, 1914. Following the First World War, his family returned to Latvia where Dravnieks studied mechanical engineering and graduated from the University of Riga. In 1949, after the Soviet Union forcibly incorporated Latvia and its neighboring Baltic states, Dravnieks came to the United States, one of nearly 100,000 Latvians who emigrated during the era following World War II. He settled first in Chicago, then in Fort Atkinson, Wisconsin, and thereafter in Madison. For the last ten years, Dravnieks has resided in Thiensville, just north of Milwaukee, where he continues to pursue his engineering profession.

Latvians, alternately beset by the German and Russian empires, have long been concerned with preserving a sense of cultural identity. Since at least the early nineteenth century, they have diligently recorded their folksongs and have sought to preserve such traditional instruments as the *kokle*. One of a small, independent family of musical instruments found in the Baltic region, the *kokle* takes the form of a truncated triangle. Nine, eleven, or thirteen strings extend from a metal string bar at the narrow end of the triangle to a series of pegs at the wide end. There are no bridges or frets between the pegs and the string holder, a characteristic which distinguishes the instrument from the somewhat similar zither. Like a boat, the body of the *kokle* is carved from a single piece of wood. A separate deck or sounding board, decorated with stylized solar designs, covers the carved chamber. Laid across the lap, the instrument is played with a plectrum much like a dulcimer or zither.

Like his fellow Latvians, Konstantins Dravnieks was attracted to the *kokle* as a vehicle for expressing his ethnic identity. His interest in the instrument, however, has taken him farther than most other Latvian-Americans. In the course of his travels as an engineer, Dravnieks has visited numerous museums and documented *kokles* in their collections with the precision of a design professional. He has also mapped the distribution of the whole family of related Baltic instruments. Through his studies and research, Dravnieks eventually came in contact with Leonids Linauts of Reading, Pennsylvania, who showed him how *kokles* are made. Inspired by Linauts, Dravnieks attempted to make a *kokle* in 1961. His first efforts proved successful and he has continued making the instruments to the present. Dravnieks has made over eighty *kokles* in all and frequently exhibits his work at *kokle* festivals and other Latvian events.

True to his engineering background, Konstantins Dravnieks has experimented almost continually with the materials, design, and dimensions of the *kokle*. Generally he builds his bodies out of maple or basswood, two kinds of wood indigenous to Latvia but also readily available in American lumberyards. His sounding boards are crafted of European spruce, and his pegs are carved from exotic and slip-resistant cocobolo wood. For strings, Dravnieks has found that music wire is the simplest, cheapest and best material.

All the instruments that Konstantins Dravnieks has crafted have been carefully recorded through the creation of precise rubbings. In his development of these renderings, Dravnieks follows his inclination to research and documentation, while providing his Latvian community with a ready record of the body of work created by one of its best known instrument-makers.

Beautifully crafted
kokles and Latvian
newspapers reflect
Dravnieks' ethnic
heritage.

WANG CHOU VANG
Menomonie, Wisconsin

Bamboo Flutes, Hmong Violins

Vang plays a Hmong bamboo flute in his Menomonie, Wisconsin home.

"I left my mother and father behind, and I'm lonely in this country and nobody helps."

Following the close of the Vietnamese War, thousands of Hmong refugees fled their Laotian homeland. After spending extended periods in refugee camps in Thailand, many Hmong refugees eventually resettled in the United States. Large concentrations of Hmong immigrants developed in California, Washington, Pennsylvania, Minnesota, North Carolina, Massachusetts and Wisconsin. Presently, Wisconsin's Hmong population is about 20,000, with sizeable communities located in Sheboygan, Eau Claire, La Crosse and Milwaukee.

Prior to their arrival in the United States, Hmong women won widespread recognition for the impressive needlework they created in the Thai camps and sold through various religious and social service organizations. Skills that they had once applied to the creation of elaborate belts, collars and bags for their traditional costumes were now utilized to create decorative *paj ntaub,* or "flower cloths," for an American market. Their beautiful batik, applique, reverse applique and embroidery soon took such variant forms as wall hangings, pot holders, doilies, coasters and eyeglass cases.

While Hmong women were garnering high praise from American audiences for their craft skills, many Hmong men were frustrated by the various difficulties which kept them from pursuing their traditional handcrafts in the United States. Blacksmiths, jewelers, and instrument-makers in their native Laos, Hmong men in this country were unable to afford the silver necessary for traditional necklaces and bracelets and unable to find the right kinds of bamboo for flutes and other instruments. Nonetheless, a number of Hmong craftsmen, including Wisconsin's Wang Chou Vang, have continued to pursue their callings against these considerable odds.

Born in Laos in 1952, Wang Chou Vang came to the United States in 1980, settling first in Elk Mound and then in Eau Claire. As a boy, Vang learned to play the *nkauj nrog ncas,* or two-stringed violin, and the bamboo flute. Both instruments were used in courting and in the traditional Hmong New Year's celebrations. In addition, Vang recalled that he would use the flute and violin to play music upon entering a village during wartime. The songs he played indicated who he was and that he came in peace.

In Laos, Vang made two-stringed violins for sale to other musicians. Since coming to the United States, he has made only a few for his own use. In constructing these, Vang has had to find suitable substitutes for various unavailable materials. He has, for example, been forced to use metal cylinders and gourds for the soundboxes of the violins. He has also come to cover the resonators with the hides of raccoon or deer he has hunted. Though it has sometimes been difficult to obtain, Vang has usually been able to get horsehair for the bow of his two-stringed violins, and he has also continued to carve an Asian bird, an *aum vaag,* at the end of the instrument's neck. Thus, despite considerable obstacles, Wang Chou Vang has successfully contributed to the preservation of Hmong music in Wisconsin and the United States through dedication to his traditionally male craft of instrument-making.

Wang Chou Vang
holds one of his
traditional two-
stringed violins.

MIGUEL CRUZ
Milwaukee, Wisconsin

Cuatros, Guiros, and Maracas

Miguel Cruz was born in 1936 in Aguas Buenas, Puerto Rico. His father was a farmer and, like his father before him, a *cuatro*-maker. The *cuatro* is a plucked lute of the guitar family strung with five sets of double-course strings. It is used by the Spanish-Indian population of Puerto Rico to play *musica jibara* on Saturday nights and during the year-end holiday season. Miguel's father, Juan Cruz, cut local timber for his *cuatros* and shaped them using hand tools. He used glue made by boiling the native *pinuela* plant to fasten his instruments together. Miguel learned to make *cuatros* by watching his father work, and he also learned to play both *cuatro* and guitar while growing up in Puerto Rico.

Miguel Cruz came to Wisconsin in 1958, and over the years he has earned a living doing factory work. Around 1965, motivated by a desire to keep family and community traditions alive, Cruz began to make *cuatros* based upon his recollection of his father's

techniques. Like his father, Miguel Cruz painstakingly shapes his instruments with saws, files, chisels and clamps. However, he has been forced to find alternative sources for certain of the materials necessary for his instruments. Instead of cutting local timber for his wood, Cruz scavenges wood from old dressers and chest-of-drawers destined for the dump. He uses white pine and salvaged mahogany for the sides and necks of his *cuatros* as well as cow bones from a local butcher for the bridge and the nut. Strings, pegs and gears he purchases from a music store. In place of the *pinuela* plant favored by his father, Cruz uses Elmer's Glue. Despite the variant sources of his materials, Miguel Cruz finishes his instruments in the manner traditional in Puerto Rico. He coats the light-colored tops of his *cuatros* with a clear finish and backs, sides and necks with a dark varnish.

In addition to making *cuatros* for the Milwaukee Puerto Rican community, Miguel Cruz repairs and rebuilds older guitars and *cuatro* and fashions simple percussion instruments like *guiros,* or gourd scrapers, and *maracas.* His instruments are usually sold as fast as he can make them. A performer as well as an instrument-maker, Cruz also takes part in the seasonal serenading with which the Puerto Rican community marks the end of the year. Through his instrument-making and his playing, Miguel Cruz continues a generations-old family tradition and contributes to the preservation of his community's rich array of holiday customs.

Miguel Cruz's kitchen table doubles as a workbench for his cuatro-building.

In addition to building cuatros, Miguel Cruz repairs and restores the traditional Puerto Rican instruments. Cruz removed the back and deepened the body of this cuatro.

WILLIAM SCHWARTZ

Sheboygan, Wisconsin

"Stumpf Fiddles"

Bill Schwartz displays a "Stumpf fiddle" in the showroom of his Sheboygan promotional marketing firm.

Bill Schwartz moved to Green Bay with his family at a very early age. As a boy, he was given a toy consisting of a short stick to which a number of percussive noisemakers were attached. Schwartz not only played with the rhythm stick as a child, but resurrected it in the early 1970s for use in Shriners' parades. Attired as an enormous rabbit, Schwartz would clown around behind marching bands, mimicking their tempos with his music stick.

At roughly the same time, while attending a Green Bay Packers game, Schwartz encountered two brothers from Sheboygan shaking a larger, more elaborate version of his own noisemaker whenever the home team fared well. Not long after this chance encounter, the same two brothers happened to seek out Schwartz, a professional marketing consultant, to assist them in selling their rhythm stick. They had already dubbed the instrument the "Stumpf Fiddle" after a

mythical peg-legged tippler by the name of Harry Stumpf who stomped the floor with his wooden leg while sipping beers. After talking with the Cronin brothers, Schwartz placed an ad in the Wall Street Journal for $600, received $10,000 worth of orders, and found himself in business with the pair.

The Stumpf Fiddle, as designed by the Cronins and modified by Schwartz, consists of a metal shaft with a ball at the base and a wooden handle at the top. The shaft is outfitted with rows of jingle bells, a wood block, a taxi horn, a cast metal bell, a set of springs, a bicycle bell, and two stainless steel pie plates holding a handful of washers. The up-and-down bouncing of the shaft activates a number of the attached noisemakers, while a fiberglass beater stick is used to sound the wood block and the cast bell. Schwartz purchases the various parts which comprise his Stumpf Fiddles, then contracts with local senior citizens who assemble the instruments in their basement workshops.

Perhaps by virtue of its name, the Stumpf Fiddle retains certain of its central European associations. Also known as the "boomba" or *"Teufel* stick," the instrument remains a favorite entertainment at such celebrations as Sheboygan area "brat fries." Bill Schwartz has, however, succeeded in marketing the instrument throughout the United States and has even placed Stumpf Fiddles in the hands of Bill Cosby, Gerald Ford and Mickey Spillane. Thanks to Schwartz's mass marketing, soon no home in America will be without its very own Stumpf Fiddle!

A rack of completed
"Stumpf fiddles"
awaiting shipment in the
basement workshop of
a Schwartz employee.

CHECKLIST OF THE EXHIBITION

PAST MASTERS:

ANDREW AND GEORGE KARPEK
(1894-1942 and 1918-1988)
Piano Accordion
1930s
Wood, celluloid, steel reeds;
   c. 18½ x 15 x 8¾″
Loaned by Karpek Accordion
   Manufacturing Company

ANDREW AND GEORGE KARPEK
(1894-1942 and 1918-1988)
Accordion
1930s
Wood, celluloid, inlay;
   c. 18½ x 15 x 8¾″
Loaned by Karpek Accordion
   Manufacturing Company

EDWIN JOHNSON
(1905-1984)
Nyckelharpa (Key Harp)
1981
Wood; 35 x 9½ x 4″
From the collection of the
   Wisconsin Folk Museum,
   Mt. Horeb

EDWIN JOHNSON
(1905-1984)
Fiddle
Laminated wood; 23½ x 8 x 3½″
From the collection of the
   Wisconsin Folk Museum,
   Mt. Horeb

LOUIS PIDGEON
Menominee Lover's Flute
1928
Wood, red paint; 22″ long
From the collection of the
   State Historical Society
   of Wisconsin, Madison

Winnebago Flute
Wood, with pewter or lead bands; 21¾″ long
From the collection of the
   State Historical Society
   of Wisconsin, Madison

WISCONSIN INDIAN INSTRUMENTS:

JAMES RAZER
Tony, Wisconsin
Ojibwa Deer Toe Jingles
1989
Deer toes, fur
Loaned by the artist

LOUIS WEBSTER
Neopit, Wisconsin
Woodland Flute
1989
Wood, glue; 23½ x 3 x 1½″
From the collection of the
   Cedarburg Cultural Center,
   Cedarburg

JOSEPH ACKLEY
Lac du Flambeau, Wisconsin
Ojibwa Dance Drum
1990
Wood, buckskin, rawhide, thread,
fur; 39 x 35 x 36″
From the collection of the
   Cedarburg Cultural Center,
   Cedarburg

NORTH WOODS MUSIC MAKERS:

OTTO RINDLISBACHER
(1895-1975)
Hardanger Fiddle
Maple, ebony, spruce, mother-of-pearl,
ink; 25½ x 7¾ x 4½″
From the collection of Vesterheim,
   The Norwegian-American Museum
   Decorah, Iowa

OTTO RINDLISBACHER
(1895-1975)
Cigar Box Fiddle
Wood, cigar box, mother-of-pearl; 23 x 7 x 3″
From the collection of the
   State Historical Society
   of Wisconsin, Madison;
   Gift of Lois Rindlisbacher Albrecht

OTTO RINDLISBACHER
(1895-1975)
Cane Fiddle
Wood, metal; 35½ x 5⅞ x 2¼″
From the collection of Vesterheim,
   The Norwegian-American Museum,
   Decorah, Iowa

OTTO RINDLISBACHER
(1895-1975)
Miniature Fiddle and Chain
Bone or ivory; 1⅜ x ½ x 17″ (with chain)
From the collection of Vesterheim,
   The Norwegian-American Museum,
   Decorah, Iowa

RAY CALKINS
Chetek, Wisconsin
Cigar Box Guitar
Wood, metal strings, 36 x 8¼ x 4″
From the collection of the
Rusk County Historical Society, Ladysmith

RAY POLARSKI
Three Lakes, Wisconsin
Fiddle
1987
Spruce, hard maple, curly flamed maple,
ebony; 23 x 7½ x 3½"
Loaned by the artist

OLD WORLD INSTRUMENTS:

EPAMINONTAS BOURANTAS
Milwaukee, Wisconsin
Bouzouki
1989
Rosewood, ebony, Sitka spruce, mother-
of-pearl, acetate; 34½ x 12 x 6½"
Loaned by the artist

EPAMINONTAS BOURANTAS
Milwaukee, Wisconsin
Baglama
1989
Rosewood, ebony, Sitka spruce, mother-of-
pearl, acetate; 22 x 4¾ x 3½"
Loaned by the artist

EPAMINONTAS BOURANTAS
Milwaukee, Wisconsin
Tzoura
1989
Rosewood, ebony, Sitka spruce, mother-of-
pearl, acetate; 22 x 6 x 3½"
Loaned by the artist

ALFONSO AND IVO BALDONI
Milwaukee, Wisconsin
Baldoni 4/5 Reed Chamber Accordion
1960
Honduras mahogany, walnut, spruce,
aluminum, steel, celluloid; 21 x 17 x 10"
Loaned by A. Baldoni Music Service

BALDONI FAMILY
Castelfidardo, Italy
Ficosecco Diatonic Button Accordion
1989
Ash, maple, marquetry inlay; bellows of cloth,
cardboard, calfskin; 10 x 11 x 5½"
Loaned by A. Baldoni Music Service

ALFONSO AND IVO BALDONI
Milwaukee, Wisconsin
Polka Accordion
1930s
Mahogany, maple, spruce, aluminum, steel,
celluloid; 20 x 15 x 9¾"
Loaned by A. Baldoni Music Service

RON POAST
Black Earth, Wisconsin
Hardanger Fiddle
1989-1990
Sitka spruce, Gabon ebony, curly maple,
mother-of-pearl, abalone; 25 x 9 x 4"
Loaned by the artist

NICK VUKUSICH
Bisernica
Milwaukee, Wisconsin
1989-1990
Bird's eye maple, spruce, maple, rosewood,
ebony, abalone; 28 x 8 x 2½"
Loaned by the artist

KONSTANTINS DRAVNIEKS
Thiensville, Wisconsin
Latvian *Kokle*
1964
Basswood, spruce, hickory; 26 x 8 x 3¼"
Loaned by the artist

NEW ARRIVALS, NEW DIRECTIONS:

WANG CHOU VANG
Menomonie, Wisconsin
Hmong Two-Stringed Violin
1989
Wood, gourd, raccoon hide, metal strings,
horsehair bow; 36½ x 5½ x 4¼"
Gift of the artist to the
    Cedarburg Cultural Center,
    Cedarburg

MIGUEL CRUZ
Milwaukee, Wisconsin
Puerto Rican *Cuatro*
Wood, metal strings; repaired by the artist
Loaned by the artist

WILLIAM SCHWARTZ
Sheboygan, Wisconsin
"Stumpf Fiddle"
1990
Metal, wood, percussion instruments,
fiberglass stick; 48" high
Loaned by the artist

*Complementing the instruments featured in the
exhibition are field photographs by Lewis Koch
as well as artifacts and photographs from the
collections of Joyce Haver, Cedarburg; the State
Historical Society of Wisconsin; the Milwaukee
Public Museum; the Wisconsin Folk Museum; the
Rusk County Historical Society; the Mt. Horeb
Area Historical Society; and Vesterheim, The
Norwegian-American Museum, in Decorah, Iowa.*